Accounting for the Dark

Books by Peter Cooley

Accounting for the Dark

Peter Cooley

Carnegie Mellon University Press
Pittsburgh 2024

Acknowledgments

Certain of these poems or versions of them have appeared, sometimes titled differently, in the following magazines and the author is grateful to the editors for permission to reprint.

Bennington Review: "A Litany in Time of Plague"; *Christian Century*: "The Agony in the Garden," "Aubade" ("sometimes certain mornings"), "Down Autumn," "Fra Angelico, 'The Annunciation,' 1433-1446," "Innumerabilities," "Now"; *Commonweal*: "Besides," "Unanswered Questions," "Midas and Midas," "Friendship Intercept" ("We never know how many days we have"); *Copper Nickel*: "In the Bestiary"; *Hampden-Sydney Poetry Review*: "Devotional Images"; *The Louisville Review*: "Poem in the Third Week of Advent"; *The New Yorker*: "Bear," "The Heaven of the Vampires"; *North American Review*: "Dialogue Where I Do Little Talking"; *Image*: "Little Allegory"; *Plume*: "Mommie"; *Poetry East*: "Allegory of Sorts," "Certainties of Interchange"; *The Southern Review*: "Woundings"; *Volt*: "Hibernals," "Interrogations"; *Vox Populi*: "The Continuous Desire to be Reborn," "Company to Keep," "Keats Etc.," "The Daily Grind," "Souvenirs"; *Xavier Review*: "Gracelight," "Quarantine Alba"; *The Yale Review*: "To My Daughter"

"Jacob's Ladder," "Riven, Driven Back," "Incarnation Intercept Sonnet," "Incarnations," and "Legacy of Blue" appeared in *On the Seawall*.

"Little Allegory" appeared in *Poetry Daily* and was featured in the podcast *Loudmouth Angel*.

"Sheltering in Place" appeared in the anthology *Together in a Certain Strangeness*, Alice Quinn, Editor. New York: Knopf, 2020.

"Writing about the Stars under My Feet" appeared in *The Poetry Buffet Anthology*, New Orleans: *New Orleans Poetry Journal Press*, 2023.

Thanks to the Best Poetry Group Ever, Carolyn Hembre, Kay Murphy, Brad Richard, Andy Young, Katie Balma, Rodney Jones, Toi Derricotte, Laura Mullen, and Allison Campbell for insightful readings and suggestions.

Special thanks are due to Nicole Cooley and Rodney Jones for suggestions on this manuscript.

Book design by Jen Bortner

Library of Congress Control Number 2023951322
ISBN 978-0-88748-699-9
Printed and bound in the United States of America

10 9 8 7 6 5 4 3 2 1

for Nicole, Alissa, and Josh

Contents

One

Two

Three

One

Because we don't know when we will die, we get to think of life as an inexhaustible well. Yet everything happens only a certain number of times . . . and a very small number, really. How many more times will you remember a certain afternoon of your childhood . . . some afternoon that's so deeply a part of your being that you can't even conceive of your life without it? Perhaps four or five times more. Perhaps not even that! How many more times will you watch the full moon rise? Perhaps twenty and yet it all seems limitless.

from *The Sheltering Sky* by Paul Bowles

Little Soul

by Hadrian
translated by W. S. Merwin

Little soul little stray
little drifter
now where will you stay
all pale and all alone
after the way
you used to make fun of things

A Litany in Time of Plague

Follow the dark, the split in everything,
the silence between trees where the winds stop,
the dead birds singing an echo's echoing—

Follow the dark. Then curse while you walk through
the hands that grapple, twining about your neck
unfathomable. You'll never learn their names.

Follow the dark. There will be days,
decades you are leading, you think, you are not.
Always you are one step behind, no seven.

Follow the dark. Let its footsteps be rain,
no, rain will be the pace you cannot imitate.
Let nothing but darkness be your talisman.

Follow the dark. Ahead the raven song,
midnight unable to separate from day,
light-extinguished blooms under your foot

you cannot separate from blind horizons,
the light inside your hands, the darkness widening,
deep, impenetrable, high—follow the dark,

the dark inside your thighs, this small fire we carry
the thousands of angles of a holy lust,
that dark the inexactitude by which we live—

Prayer before Dawn in Time of the Pandemic

There is community for me in the morning light
I cannot find among communities of the human
man or woman, but in the trees when morning comes to each
according to ability or need or petition from their branches,
light undressing them from the top down, stripping last night's
    stars—
once they stand naked, I pray my naked words.
It's all about starting again again—

I have a firmament where I discard my prayers:
it's my other community. They call it wind
who chart the weather. The ancients feared its spirits.
I'm with them, but mine embraces me.
I call it heaven, I'm in its summer's susurrus,
the murmur of the portals permitting entrance
even as I start to carve these words—
they came to me from voices in myself
belonging to others I still haven't met,
voices of my own, rending, mending me more riven—

Covid 19: The Third Week in New Orleans

My friends cover Facebook with dead news.
Iowa City, New York, Chicago,
who craves more fear? I don't read what they write.
Poets, fiction writers, artists, professors,

why don't they send me words close to their pulse?
But since I'm always ravenous for connection
I can't resist these photographs they post—
images become afterimage, stumbling here.

Spring's beginning! And not only on my street,
but rank continuance swelling its buds—
through dogwood, magnolia, adagios of blossoming
sounding Chicago, deserted, empty New York.

Even evergreens shimmer some new difference,
they, too, having a place in this persistence,
firs, Norfolk Pine, the sky wrapped in their boughs,
leaf-on-leaf, the full screen, while I scroll.

How tenuous, my sweat printing the smartphone
as I frame this, how fungible our fractured language
evolving fear into these pictures of our churning world,
insisting as they roil, we go on, insisting—

Sheltering in Place

New Orleans, April 2020

Sweet peas on my coffee table insist they start this poem.
Once they might have called up a painting by Monet,
but today they're just some image of mortality
I snipped quickly from my neighbor's front yard fence
after, shaking, I read her note "Please, please,
take." Covid-19, we're sheltering-in-place.
I jog around the block, she walks to work,
Emergency NICU nurse at our neighborhood hospital.

Over there, somebody's being born, somebody's dying.
somebody's being tested. How much, this minute,
I crave the sweet pea odor of transfiguration.
The cut flowers' scent is just rusted garden shears.

I savor my sense of smell. I'm well, I'm safe at home.
Reader, help my tongue—taste these flowers' hues:
piquant crimsons, tart amethysts, honey-ambers.

While I've been writing here, someone over there died.

Collateral Angels

appear, as always, uninvited,
this time as constellations in my backyard
grazing the live oaks, then, lightning
traversing the window of my living room,
instantaneously setting the house on fire.

Today once more I have to follow, Peter,
the fourth Wise Man, treading imagination,
no wiser, just very practiced
at transcendence, as we have to call this.
I believe in what they followed to believe
to return some unknown way. Fungibility!
Collateral angels today when I allow them.
when I have faith in wings, the nimbus,
as long as I subscribe to the unseen.

Aubade

Sometimes, certain mornings, we are born again,
our feet traveling the floor new feet, new floor,
our windows watching us as we cat-stretch, all new

to see our yard staring, blossoming,
these flowers we planted yesterday
more wide-eyed than when we put them to bed.

We've never seen such hue regard the sky,
every impatiens' uplifted head
jubilant, defiant, red, on red, on red.

After such streaming light come to our hands
like stigmata to the saints, we shower and wait,
the old terror, our familiar, on its way—

the shaving or the make-up mirrors will hold
our bones a death mask fits, then mirror back our yards—
nothing the same color, nothing, sun's every glance.

Listening to Seamus Heaney Read Beowulf While Crossing the Bonnet Carré Spillway Toward New Orleans

Ahead, the spillway's end, and when I'm there,
after the battle, Heaney's plosives, vowels,
hewn out of Irish history and exile,
Beowulf will die.

          No, he's dying right now!
I wasn't listening carefully, was I?
And I still have a couple hundred yards
to make myself one with the passing sun,
flickering here, there, here.
                              Yes, I can do this.
All it takes is absolute surrender.

Now the sun from the seventh century
alive on the unknown author, dying,
alive on Heaney with his Irish vowels,
blinds the windshield, I'm driving into it—

Woundings

Layers of fear. They were like morning clouds,
stratus formations lined up over the river,
the Mississippi stalling at the end of my street.

Scaling the embankment, I reached the levee road.
Forty years I've stood here, waiting for God.
Sure enough, a god was here, and right on time,

His, mine, a compromise between us.

The bikers and the joggers had to pass—
I waited for another pack of runners.
I stepped out of their determinations.

Now. No one's around to watch me reach down

into the wounded, through sun-dipped levee grass.
The gull, both wings broken, warms my palms.
Home again, I can still feel the heart pulsing,

writing this, while I release him on his journey
again, for both of us, down, into the Mississippi.

Golden Hour

My little happiness, these sparrows, not Williams'
"shrill piping of plenty" in his street but mine
has come to my late afternoon's despair
to drink in chorus at the terra-cotta saucer
encircling the snake plant on my stoop.
New Orleans, late August Covid-19—

This ailing, dun-tipped plant is a little less sick
than I am, knowing exactly what it needs
while the golden hour begins its dance around us.

Warbling choir slung around the saucer.
I never asked for this, transcendence stuck
to my shoe bottoms as I go out, lifting the ground
for a late afternoon run around the block.
I'd planned to water the plant, but I won't now
since this whole heaven-thing has inched me up a bit.

I'm going to let that predicted rain tonight,
churning the sky right now, swell the plant's saucer.
Memory, I know those birds will never come again.

Jacob's Ladder

My soul has taken in the clear, cold light
paradise offers when we have lost enough—
parents, lovers, children, friends, directions back—

then we are alone with the Alone again,
our witness to all things we find in changingness.

Aloneness has its own music, it digs in heels
to ladders lowered from the unseen clouds.
It raises wings to scale the rungs, ascend, descend—

musics we've never heard, angels expressionless
until we face them, choose to give one face.

What profiles we exchange then in our rise and fall!
What company we keep! Am I going up or down?
Transversals, circles, zigzags, parallelograms?

Alternate Canonical Prayer

Because some things just can't be said, this will be song.
Certain mornings, my dead return to me,
mother, sister, father, gone in one year,
year the rupture of the millennium
and last year, You, Love, never waking up
that morning I found you, touched your cold forehead.

But this has to be said. I never cry for them
to come back yet they come, the sky in motion,
clouds that insist on passing, their transit
dumb allegory of the mortal life.

I don't pick them out, one by one.
They're all a part, apart, together.
They rivet the sky, enclose its tops and sides.

This morning I'm confident they're watching me,
maybe giving me these words to pray?
After all, this started as a prayer.
Now's it's continuance I can't separate from clouds,
words I've pulled down from the mortal passing,
their presence, their gifts to me, ragged syllables
punning on presents-presence stupidly.

However badly I'm shaking this out,
it means you've spoken through me, all of you.
Because some things just can't be said, I sing.
Mortal, afraid of my own words, I'm still alive.

The Agony in the Garden

Raphael, Italian, (Urbino) 1483–1520, tempera and oil on wood

How happily I, Saint Peter, slept, beside the others
while Christ sweated blood, asking The Father
to take the cup from Him. And then—He never asked—
the angel came, the angel strengthened Him,
positioned in the sky, wings of flame.
Now I pass the poem, oranged with fire,
to my namesake, Peter Cooley.
He'll tell you why you're reading this.

Thanks, Saint Peter. It's that angel
first in the text, Luke 22:39-46, then in the painting,
I don't need to call down, ever.
The orange burns, a cleansing.
I put my face against the fire.
There is a way such images really happen.
There is a way this is not ekphrasis.

When I am trying to pray—or I am prayed.
for the world's contagions, 2021,
I look up, the angel waits. Always, all along,
orange of a lit match, unfurling wings.
Even He needed to be strengthened.

Besides

there's never-heaven always in my hand
reminding me my fingers have no grip
on Heaven ever, coming through the trees—

that kind of fastening the morning holds
on everything the sun allows to pass
under surveillance, possession, loss, loss, loss . . .

Once I thought I was here to name the stars.
Wasn't that yesterday? But now I know
in this blue moment I'll find everything.

I could invent the jaybird in my yard
but he is singing. That's how I fly from here—
already he is more than I can bear,

his music tearing me up inside till I die,
rise, die, rise, die. This is just a metaphor.
And this: I'm resurrected every day.

Twice Last Night I Saw Eternity

—after Henry Vaughan

The second time it was that smaller light
a flashlight flickers, battery almost dead
but these mazurkas lit up the Western sky
each instant panoramic, grace dechained from asking,
the declaration of a wish fulfilled
such as the full moon scatters with its silence
on the darkest dark waters at summer's end.

The first time I experienced it in Braille
though I'm 20/20 with glasses and the shell
I stooped to reach along the beach stood still
seconds before the ground under my step
curved outward, the surface of another world.

I was the shell and on the shell.
In the interior I whorled, my own echo,
my soul, the shell. There was an angel,
a fistful of wings. I'll have to tell you
the rest tomorrow. When you are more receptive.

Blue Sopranos

How sweet to drink the music now first light
of my familiars, the sparrows in the street,
this warble of their voices ravenous

to call me out. Shhh. I'll never whisper our secret
to anybody else. Believe me.
Listen, in this blue air, most ordinary of men,

cursing the newsman tossing my paper on my lawn
the middle of some dogwalker's accustomed gift,
I'm not who I am. And sparrows wait, all preparation.

I let my music, the undersong I keep
rolled up, release its tenor with my wings.
I'm here, midair, pinions among their number—

Have you come with me this far? Can I say:
You have your minutes as accompaniment?
Our mornings we're just notes strewn on the wind?

Carrion Cry, Mayfly Lament

I

Instead of the morning shining in all things
I'll choose the shadows, the undersides today,
to light my way as only darkness can,

clarity of opposition in its wings.

I'll be the carrion caught up in flight
that buzzard transcribes. Will it be beak or claw
to carry me, to drop me when he dies

when we both fall, our descent ravaging?

Our faith is this descent I make up for my wings,
spreading their pinions the second I'm alone.
Below me, as the day proceeds, those shadows,

shadows he taught me, caught up, agonized.

II

The tiniest of the afternoon's mayflies
gifts me with shadow, now his final hour.
Both of us know this minute his last shadowing,

I'll bifurcate, cut up in squares or sixteenths,

minute perspectives I look down on flying past,
his little shadow illuminating rubies,
emeralds, the cityscape of glittering

light of the twilight, jeweled in the night,
the fly and I brothers, cousins to light.
But I chose the darkness. Or was I chosen?

In My Soul These Things Occurred to Me It Was Not a Matter of My Choosing

Christmas Eve the incarnations can proceed,
the gold-stippled first light on the live oaks
along my street taking the miracles
for granted and why not and then the front windows
of every house on Harding, 243, next to me, 245, etc.
And now the garbage scow, the gold-encrusted truck—

why do these men have to work this special evening?—
their hopping on and off more gold and now they heave
my can, of course gold, and pass the dog walkers,
greeting each other as they pass, a little incarnation clot,
their gold panning gold, the pillage spilling,
the Irish Wolfhound, and three mongrel pups, a goldest gold.

The spiral notebook from Shopper's Value, blinding, gold
under my fingers as I write, closing my eyes,
I widen my gaze on new satieties.
I write this in the book of miracles.

Obit of Sorts

It's just a little exultation,
well, sort of a miniature,
but will have to do,
to get me through today,
the black rain of the afternoon
after the news of my friend's suicide,
leaving behind a wife
of twenty years, daughters, ten,
thirteen, the selfish bastard I loved.
Now this sudden light inside me
I think will get me through the maelstrom
every window of my soul,
while the New Orleans weather
shines, October-gold,
shot through with crystalline.
What gifts these are, the exaltations,
these liftings, I don't even ask,
I'm ascended, one foot at a time,
the same step of the unknowable,
hope, monotonous, the air clearing.
I'm here, the horizon lifts its wings.
I'm traveled, traveling,
I think the stars inside
Know where I'm going, where I am—

Christmas Morning, the Magi

Because they always must return another way,
The Three, they miss every year
all the rest of the story. Small wonder how the story unfolds:
centuries roll by while we reconstruct,
deconstruct, the cross, the resurrection.

I find myself—only this morning, now—
in their transparency. Once they saw, they believed,
the star inside corresponding to the heaven-seen.

As a kid, my family sequestered The Magi.
I was forbidden to play with them, I sneaked
fingers into the box, knocked a triple-header
together, chipped all three in the closet's dark.

When I remember, I know how to pray.
We have our wounds, we never asked for them.

Afterlight

When I return to earth I'll be no man.
I think I'll have my own choice of trees, don't you?
I'll come back this willow below the levee road,
half in, half out of the Mississippi.

Katrina took it, shook it, to still stand,
dangling those fluted leaves across the waves,
this plashing so melodious it sounds made up
until the wind accompanying me begins.

I'll want to come back to be this music—

But if earth won't have me, I'll be the sky,
a cloud dissolving, to reform, some shape
a boy-man like myself might reimagine.
Today it's lion, unicorn, a herd of deer

which, even as I speak, transform again—

Now,

after a first moment in eternity
I turn around. I'm back in my backyard,
the weeping willow dead, the bottle brush,
the southern flowers I planted, novelties
to me, the northerner, dead, dead, all dead.

And on the branches of the dead magnolia
the dead birds perch, swallow and nightingale,
their dead eyes holding reflections of the flowers,
genus and species, dead, sere, leaves cracked, dead
all crawling things, all flying, speechless, dead,

waiting and hollowed out with harrowing.
I lay my hand among these shadowings.
Because she always answered, I choose her,
this mockingbird. I sing her my first word.
The rest is heaven, endlessness of grace.

Innumerabilities

Morning. I watch the windows come to light—
each according to ability or need or willingness—

in my east-facing living room. I wait.
Too soon this time will pass. Minutes from now

today arrives, I'll have to be one man
to my dead wife and children, everyone I meet.

But now the windows' musics no one hears
but the angels passing for their moments

across these panes. Let me count them.
How many can I number, Heaven as it transpires

I say to the third angel, the one I pull down now,
the one who blesses and is blessed

with fire dancing on the page, invisible,
the heat I've taken into my fingers, tongue—

tongue, fingers, angel-light, blue windows turning gold—
how else might I go out against the world?

Writing about the Stars under My Feet

I'm singing to the blue jay in my yard
who never sang to me but will today

if I feather him a new blue enough—

Listen, he's playing the "Hallelujah Chorus"
from the *Messiah*, assigning me a part.

Before I leave, for one of the upper branches
in the unseen, just let me question

what kind of God comes to me every day
in forms I never see till I raise wings

from the unknowns I'm lifting here, right now.

Christ-of-this-moment, Christ-of-I-hope-the-next,
what difference is there between I and me,

Christ-in-us to sing, shouting out the new man
I am, the blue jay's promise, invisible.

Two

Since our apparitions, the part of us which appears, are so momentary compared with the other, the unseen part of us which spreads wide, the unseen might survive, be recovered somehow attached to this person or that, or even haunting certain places after death . . . perhaps—perhaps.

—Virginia Woolf, *Mrs. Dalloway*

Incarnation Intercept

We only have so many of these days,
I said to the sparrow, who is my nightingale,
I repeated to the wasp always my patient spider,
I chanted to the frog, my narrow fellow in the grass.
Then, armed with John, and Walt and Emily,
I could begin the day again as they have taught,
the sky inside me corresponding with the sun's.

This is the other side of my dark night,
this New Orleans seamless blue, this vast surround
where I have earned my trade, license to kill
the demons who would populate my fists.
It is this simple: I open both my hands,
gesture of supplication to the gods
I make up quickly to steer me through the day,
gods I will bring down to one, invisible,
oarsman through my black water's Acheron.
I'm still in Avernus here. I can't change that.

Mayfly Colloquy

"I'm just here to start another poem,"
the Mayfly says, flapping its pinions

across my left forearm, where I can take in
splendiferous wings weighted with dawnings.

"But then," Mayfly continues, "I brought back
a line you left my progenitors,

'in the company of strangers, myself,'
the last phrase in your first book, remember?"

I don't much like it anymore, I tell the bug
and, if I'm not wrong, you have just today

to watch me while I lift these wings,
the ones I discover when I need the sky,

the new mansions up there, the jeweled rooms,
above my cellars of broken wordlessness.

My wings take off, I want the Mayfly following.
"The only way 'to' is 'through'," M. sings

off-key, sententiously, and which of us
is the more platitudinous,

I think, but I don't say it aloud,
already in the ruby room, the emerald,

a third cloud, fourth firmament, the next infinite—

Friendship Intercept

We never know how many days we have
until the call goes out to us, wordless,
the crow says, cawing on my morning run,

caw-caw-caw-cawing, breaking up the run—
But, of course, he doesn't say that, cawing.
The melody, obstreperous monotony,

breaks open spaces in me I despise,
mountain paths through my cold jugular
I have to find new lyrics for, sky-morning-wide—

The crow is gone, perched on some neighboring street—
We never know how many days we have
I repeat to the wind, old friend holding my name

summer into fall, into oblivion.
And, shouting it, the street opens ahead,
star-morning-wide, its only end these stars.

Weather Report

How can we love the dead
when their love for us
exceeds mortal expectations?
Another morning the clouds insist
on taking shape, cumulous, stratus, cirrus, cumulous
as my mother, sister, father, and my wife,
the dead churning in new configuration
minute by minute, disguised as animals
I saw there as a kid, elephant,
giraffe, lion, wing-spread duck.
I think they never loved me
enough until now
and this is my punishment
to be loved by the formless and the formed
always in motion, love always new.
How can I, even begin to answer back?
Now the sky clears. I tell myself
this was all imagination. Why not?
My faith in God is this changingness
I walk through, heaven enough
to keep me going. And they're all gone,
the vault is clear blue, streaked
by some sky writing, indecipherable,
advertising a New Orleans festival,
probably, a new restaurant, what is it?
I'll want to go there, order
something new, different,
something to take away,
this longing I have no name for.

Short Story

Christmas came and went,
the star retired
to its accustomed fix
in the mythology.
The stores reopened
to display disparity
gifts allow, and the poor
returned to poverty—
their accustomedness—
though they never left.
And I, in wonder,
wander gold aisles
astonishments keep opening
in my continuing belief
the star is in my pocket
twice, one in my wallet,
back pocket, then the brighter,
my right front pocket
where I can access it
when I plunder loose change
or my key chain. It burns
a little at first each time
I put my hand to it
since each plunge is the first
like the way it was—
that first time—
every time—I fell in love.
No, more like each time
I cross the place in myself
where the long-loved
and five-year dead one
passes discursively,

winding, winging,
taking you with her
whether or not you want it,
but this is not transcendence,
is it, your exhausted subject,
just grief, naked
unaskingness.

Alternate Devotional

Readers, it's up to you
to discover your own way
however bent, occluded,
however desperate, to walk yourself
through your mortal lives
the next few seconds—

In my own waking terrors
I return, repeatedly
to Gérard de Nerval
accompanying his fabled lobster
along the Champs-Élysée
on a string, just one
of my dawn avatars.
Then we can start morning prayer,
Gerard on the one hand,
lobster on the left, rubescent,
and there's nowhere,
in this threesome, our words
can't travel through the next
few minutes, hours even.
We are all transported,
out of time, transcendent,
sanctified, beyond poetry,
Gerard, the lobster, me.

In the Bestiary

All figurations of the morning stars
nothing but midnight light invisible—

why that's enough to start any day—
whatever lies beyond me mine to seize

as soon as I can write it here, right-sized.
I see you've started with the grandiose,

Nightingale sings, his face against the glass,
the morning window where I come for words,

some streak of heaven thrown across the floor
even on a gray day, today, my starting point.

The Grandiose, as if you had a perch
with me in immortality of flesh.

You know I have only to sing one note,
all of your little poems can't compete.

I have prehistory running in my blood.
I draw the curtains. He can't bear the dark.

The bird knows he's just myself at twice-removed
and these words just once-removed, each line.

He's just one of my devils, one of my animals.
I have multitudes. And now the poem.

Sunday Mornings

I've never found another name for Heaven
except heaven-here—this walk around the block—
our meeting-place-between we live our lives,
terra infirma, the green planet, my summer morning
New Orleans awakens today, just for me.

Little gods—the sun caught on a leaf,
the iridescence shimmering its gold,
the magnolia's fallen instant in my hand
as sun encases both of us, seconds—
all documentary of the eternal.

Citizen, I wanted you to know
theologies, but I have lost my way
in stars again, come down as fallen leaves,
two, three, the ground churning with four, five, six,
these tiniest of gods I name, rename

by close inspection, my nose to the dirt—
aphid, dung beetle, sprung rhythm of the bees,
their countless resurrection, deaths, rebirths.

I Say

it's there. I'm walking around the block now.

Gold in the upper branches of the trees,
of course, but wilder, richer inside stars
the sidewalk opens as I lift my feet,

then set them down on hues no one has seen
except the ant, the grub, the angelworm.
They have no need for mirrors in their dark—
they know themselves by fastenings they displace—

as I do, every minute I'm awake,
even in these lines, given by them to me.
They take their reassurance from the ground
I crave in others, looking in their eyes.

The Heaven of the Vampires

If our name is put up by a member,
the club is never done looking us over
our whole lives—though they have years;
their red eyes dwindle like fireflies
flickering summer, and the arch of their brows
is a moth eating into the curtains
over the bed with a night air
we take for our breath, dropping off,
or a change in the weather.

Weird we should imagine them furry,
yawns foul as an old mutt's,
gat-toothed, from Grand Guignol,
a childhood Freud dug up,
or Jung. They're nothing mythic.
Their secret is discreet, exquisite,
was tragic long ago. So we inherit it
only that last night, finally,
where our face runs with the mirror
into its masque—animal, almost comic.

Till then, believe in their manners,
distance, a respect for good taste,
that certain elevation of the head.
Their assurance of another life,
its élite, well-bred and dressed,
later is indisputable,
should they let you in. The world's last gentlemen.

Alba

I take my morning coffee with these birds,
the cacophonous unbending first light symphony.

What next do these folded wings plan to deploy
out of the sun-splayed horizon around my yard?

What will they ask of the hour after this,
of noon, then the evening's sure diminishings?

I rub my whole sweat-drenched palm
across last night stuck to both my cheeks,

streaks of midnight's crying that won't come off.
It is April, spring, beginning again.

Here, New Orleans, my choir may be plotting
departure, migration back up North.

It may take weeks to arrange new melodies.
Why, then, do I sing-shot my birds with words?

They're still at it, every moment new.
They go on, heralding, on, incessant.

Down Autumn

Down autumn, through the black trees blacker
after the rains, the trees that long to speak
but only utterances we lift from them
sufficient if they are broken as we are—

down the long corridors of frost and stippling light,
manacles of stars hugging our sides,
down afternoon, down midnight, down hours until dawn,
we lie awake, anticipation's aftermath—

Mother of Frost, Mother of Mother Earth,
Mother of Inconsolables, what song is this
we cannot hear but break in two for wonder?

Mother-October, ripe beginning of winter-spring,
take me in, cocoon me, then unwind
uncertain resurrection's certainties—
certain resurrection's uncertainties—

Death Comes to the Banquet Table

Giovanna Martinelli, Italian, c. 1630–1640, New Orleans Museum of Art

Skeletal shadow, Death
sketches the right corner,
focal point of a meager
interrupted feast.
Only the three women, center,
know how to take him in,
the eldest, blue mantled,
blanches, Is it for me?
Not yet, not yet!
The two men, left, cower manfully,
the younger dropping his scimitar.
And that banquet, fruit, bread,
was it ever touched? Everything
perfect diagonals in composition.

No one of us will merit
such preparation,
such banqueting, good company.
My mother, father, sister, and my wife,
everyone, prepared to die alone,
I know. I was there
to witness their own alones.

Hibernals

There are the days the stars remember us,
the others when they can't recall our names.
And in-between the ordinary hours,
today, for instance, when the heavens come down,
only reveal their features in the hues,
the ever-changingness, snow-fracturing,
it tells me to pour down on all things seen.

New Orleans June. Everywhere snow dots snow.
I'm here in Jackson Square where sky's white breath
enlarges the cathedral's face, the flakes
lifting the pigeons' pinions to shine gold.
I've never seen a church, a bird, before.

Forty-eight years here, this is my visit
to the old city. January summer.
I have to keep my new man changing this.

Bear

Twenty, on a Paris backstreet I took in a bear
brought out to entertain our gathering crowd.

I shit you not I say in my language of that time,
this really, really, happened. Snouted

declawed, castrated probably, he danced
on hind feet to the musics of a short whip.

Twenty, a student whose bad French was his worst pain
since he had a childhood he couldn't remember

and he told everyone that he was happy.
That was before three friends overdosed,

four more were suicides, before
we lost a child and in twelve months

I lost my mother, father, sister,
before analysis brought my childhood back—

abused by my sister until I had that pain
liquidated, in the words of the kind witch doctor.

"I had to puke," I said to the girl I was with that night,
a bid for the quick sex of her understanding.

"He kept on dancing, dancing, bleeding, dancing."
"Poor baby," she said. She was nineteen.

Where is she now? Years back, I heard: L.A.,
married, three kids, like me. I have these nights

like tonight, again, the bear comes back
to make me wonder: does she read my poetry?

Probably not. Does she remember me,
she was nineteen, probably not, poor baby.

Dialogue Where I Do Little Talking

Another of the stars I came to with my name
said I will have to wait awhile for a new one.

But it will come, dark-shining, as if you'd died
and risen, reborn. And you will wear it

like your Lone Ranger mask, remember?
Of course! No one could see my eyes,

and I was five, I could take in everything!
Now we're talking, the star said, star invisible

star by my side mornings when I get up,
star here beside me, as I fall asleep.

It's not how we gods aspire to appear
the star said, but it's your way to give us light,

and you know you have mornings of constellations
without your choosing, here-a-star, there-a-star,

the incarnation dark as accompaniment
if you agree, and how can you refuse,

you, the melody and the invented instrument?

Incarnation Intercept

Dickinson called it Eden, I would call it Stars,
this place our souls fly to for revenge.
She'd call it balm, I'd call mine darkness-lit,
revenge for the world's wounding,
she would call agony, I call memory,
the pain we've put away, mine from childhood,
hers from—well, she'll have to tell you herself
when we three meet eventually, beyond
in that next doorway, Dickinson and I call Heaven.

I think when she and I meet face-to-face
we'll exchange beasts, my minotaur for her snake,
her alabaster chambers for my tents in clouds
or maybe not face-to-face but back-to-back,
imagining the other's countenance
this side of the rite of white election.
Just touching enough to maintain us, facelessly
as the eternities unroll, the three
of us, Emily, you, reader, and me, your site
to circumambulate and all of us
counting millennia backwards
without number. Eternities do that.

Elegy: For George Floyd

I

I wake to my own breath. I touch my chest.
Now, after five years, this ache across my breathing
I can't stop carrying. Five years ago,
waking up to my wife dead, our love,
fifty-six years together in the world.

Yesterday, at noon, I turned on the TV
to check the weather, the New Orleans virus count.
I could not leave the funeral while I breathed.
On every channel weeping, thunderheads of hymns,
a woman wailing while she shook the stage,
men clutching each other as they prayed,
the name of Jesus heat lightning forked among them.
The Revered Al Sharpton, calling down God,
raising his fists across four centuries.
Reader, is it repeated on your screen right now?
Maybe the world changed. Can I say that?
No, it's not my place. May I ask this?
I am my breath. You yours. This minute
the wind, calm and green, New Orleans noon,
winds around my house, listens while I sing.
Out there, the virus. It has its own life.
Later, when I go out, I have to mask,
even if it fogs my vision, stifles breath.

II

Eight minutes forty-two seconds kneeling on his neck.
Somewhere in there, a voice calling, Mama.
Eight minutes forty-two seconds down until his breath was gone.
Sky of the world beyond imaging
listened all yesterday. The sky roars
after something like this for a time.
A time can be a little while or not.
Still, there is roaring. Sometimes the roaring
expunges the name that started it.

Sometimes the roaring stops to wonder
Is anyone listening? pausing just a minute.
Then it decides, so what? and roars on, decades.
And then the name George Floyd disappears,
returns a year or two, then soars out to the wind,
and everyone at the funeral, and Derek Chauvin,
and you and I, reader, and all the poems of this moment,
the funeral home, the cemetery, join that wind.
It's not my place, but maybe the world changed.

Can I ask that? I think the world changed.
And the roaring out there, continuance, wind, breath.

Plummage

Every morning I die into my life.
I start with the usual meanderings,
The Our Father, The St. Francis Prayer,
My first reminders I'm alive.

Then, always, I remember the living dead.
Today, in my head, it's Frans Hals'
Young Man with a Skull (Vanitas).
He's about my grandson's age, twenty-one.

I remember—the future everything.

The skull, the skull, it outsizes his head,
positioning in his right hand, a fringe of teeth
with nothing to masticate but perishings.
On his hat, a gigantic, orange, phallic

drooping feather, protrudes, his ballast.
What can Death say to such comical,
juvenile, sanguine, hopeless pretension,
a costume that might please my grandson?
You know what Death says. Hals says it all.

At Shoppers' Value

I walk through 7 a.m.'s aisles. And nobody
here except the cashiers, I hail all three,
with gracelight in my hand,
then on to the canned peaches, paper towels,
bologna, salami, every touch
intercepting some new light
seen for the first time.
What did I come for,
the inveterate daily shopper,
except my mortal pretense to deposit,
then get back, transfigurations?
Now fabric softener, ground beef,
hey, ground round for a treat,
then granola bars, my favorite, peanut butter.
I'll buy two packages, why, they're on sale!
I'll gift one to the squirrel I passed,
In the tree outside, coming in.
Maybe both, unwrapped. Animals have always,
unlike my friends, been willing
to take my transfigurations
and give me back theirs, shiningly.

Rogue et al.

Little rogue transcendence in one fist,
all I have to do is open it
slowly or quickly, dependence on the dangle
will lift me, guaranteed. Nothing to doubt.

Right now, I'd say slowly, I'm just half-awake,
even though I've been up five hours.
There, my hands are open, both.
But which, the right one writing this

or the helpless left that waits now, was the words
come to this page? Which bears the heft,
as if I didn't know, which is the rogue?
The hand clutching the sun but nothing else,

that's the transcendence intercept, the cupped
lifelines naked there, the fingers splayed.
Prayer takes the air. Heaven, are you ready?

Among the Errancies

Continue by just trying to be one man,
not multiplicities like the cloud cover.

Mimic the sun. It's one no matter how
gulfstream weather darkens, thickens,

dispensing promises of rain with gray.
Every day a constant, shifting paradise!

Paradise! What else to name today,
walls around the garden my breath I've blown

to circumscribe this little space that's mine?
Eve and the serpent are intertwined

with their temptation and the storied fruit
I won't be eating this time, occupied

with naming animals I've never seen.
Every day they have to be made up:

that beast with four heads, this bird with scores of wings.
I'll call those just yesterday's menagerie.

Something is coming toward me as I sing.
What new fish, fowl, or animal

will I make of this monster, naming him?

Three

All writing is resurrection.

—Robert Cording

In Memoriam

Remember me to these chrysanthemums—
no, no, the hydrangeas, their staggering blooms
surpassing the gold-fringed buttons stuck in place
while the hydrangeas stretch and flex,
never the same sky twice they're bringing down.

It's that persistent arc summer after summer
I would die into, if die I could. To be
one with such spanning reaching for its own form,
surpassing each surpassing with surpassing.

Legacy of Blue

Blue of confusion, blue of the sea at noon
summers when thunderheads build on the thin line

the horizon comes down to: blue of Mary's gown
standing beside her son in agonies

ten thousand times across the Renaissance.
None of this will give me back the man

my father was to me: blue his last chair,
a sort of Swedish modern with matching footstool.

There he sat, looking for my mother in a sky
Michigan unfurled for him eleven months

and then he left to me, like Mother, to these words.
I started with words; all words are wounds,

no, they are clouds; they refuse to hold the son.
Reader, I wanted to say: a father is every man's first man.

Mother Lode

After I'm dead, will the world remember me
as I remember my mother, morning flickering today

through the trees, especially the upper branches?
Light answering light, Audubon Park, New Orleans.

What kind of Mother was she? the page wants to know,
since it has been taught, poetry is discovered music.

Look, I'll tell you, give me a minute—stars
in transit, that what she was, radiance—

while last night's page still tries to raise a head,
its multiple faces I keep stomping down.

Was I a good mother? the light asks suddenly.
More than good, I answer, Mother, here I am, singing,

despite the agonies I put you through, hurrying,
entangling myself in more. Watch, I'm walking

where I used to run, with light, my legs fire
to carry my body through these trees, live oaks

New Orleans' ancestral, aged, own.
Legend writes they predate the birth of Christ.

Someday light will enter me entirely, Mother,
mother light, father light, my own light then.

We'll all be talking. A different conversation.

Between the Hours

—in memory of LD, RR, TD

Midafternoon, midwinter, shadows pulse,
then flinch, then rush toward their expected ends.
The trees on the horizon shift, adjust
minutely to the wind under my step.
That quivering stopping place? Only clouds know how it comes.

This is the spot where the suicides decide
they've waited long enough, conversed enough
with edges of a mirror never still,
voices strung around an exhaust pipe,
an incubus swimming the pill bottle.

Today, a solitary walk around the block
clearing my head from paying bills long overdue,
I stepped into your stopping places, I fell.
Mouth-on-my-mouth, each ghost of you took my breath,
flew off. Three times. Then I stood up.

Each time I fell and then returned I grasped
how you could choose to feel elected
by promise of perfection, breathless, wild
enough to take one step that can't step back.
Tonight, I let you go, all three of you—

dinner, sex, the news, descent down a deep sleep.
You think I need you. Please—

Souvenirs

After cremation, they gift you
ashes in a box of silver cardboard
ribboned with a bow. I can see my wife's box
five years ago, I'm holding
it here, right now. When will I recall
holding the others? Maybe never.

I have a confession to make.
The faces of my mother, father, sister,
all dead twenty-two years back—
before I identified their bodies
as law required before they could be burned—
all are my wife's. face. All of them that instant
when I took Jacki's face five years ago
and cut a lock of her still-auburn
73-year hair. Then kissed her forehead,
cold. Cold entered me.
That's the face I'm carrying inside.

But that hair. I've cloistered it
in my stud box next to cufflinks
she gave me as a wedding gift, the curls
gnarled in her engagement ring and wedding band.
I gave Jacki's ashes to our priest.
They're walled behind her name and ashes
on the columbarium in the churchyard.
On that granite wall an empty space
waits for my name to be chiseled there.
Every Sunday after Mass, in attendance,
I'm taking it all in. Sometimes, not often,
I leave a kiss along the stone.

Which of our three children will try
to preserve a piece of me: Nicole,
Alissa, or Josh, will one insist
a corpse should not be touched?
I wonder if they'll kiss me as I kissed.

Immortality Intercept

Today I am reading Sophocles' *Antigone*.
The chorus' comments glister, stars in flight,
the strophe and antistrophe all piebald,

striated with judgment and divine love
the gods pass back and forth, turn, counterturn.
But the stars are ancient, the stars are very cold.

They have little compassion for our suffering.

Antigone, her brothers, her mother, father—
we read them for a pretense of immortality.
These are the deepest sympathies the dead can claim.

Antigone, in your cavern, are you listening?
Shall I claim I can still light my little torch?
I write to walk beside you in the dark.

To My Daughter

When they escort you to my body they will burn,
when I am watching from that other country,
when you are weary of embellishments
death insists upon, the wilting pastels,
the embalming fluid running through my limbs
they'll overcharge you for, then they'll reduce the bill,
the fluid my extremities, fingers, toes, penis.

When you find only weeping is free.

Remember then how we laughed today at the chihuahua
aged as his mistress, the tiny, dog-jawed woman,
pearls, jeweled sweater, six-inch heels,
Upper East Side, NY, 82nd & Fifth.
When she stooped to scrape his poop
he went for her, he shook his matching rhinestones,
he reveled in his snap, his yack-yack-yack-yack-yack.
We had to turn away and turn away,
just departed from the Met, immortal-gorged.
I held a lamppost, weeping, laughing.

Laughter is just so much about the stars, now isn't it?
Stars who will remember us, father, daughter,
You, midlife, I, starting my seventh decade.

She dropped her little poop box when he snapped.

That's how they burned my father.
They'll take you to the corpse. You'll have to identify the corpse.

An Aporia

Occasionally, the wonderments shine, glare, too bright,
from the mountains of New Orleans my front yard,
the Alps and Rockies gracing my front steps,
quickly I retreat to my commonplace book,
the words I never write down, find in the wind.

Out of this singing no one hears but me,
Spirit, page of the air, sheer vanishments,
I say, Soulmate I make up for a friend,
out of this singing I mend my broken wing,
the one I keep folded behind my back—
wound, third wing.
                              I say, out of this singing
the music continuously expands,
sutures whose stiches itch and rip and run,
the pus and blood my testaments now southerly.

They direct me as they chose or as I bend,
no difference between the wind and me,
falling, stumbling, wounded, mending, wounding,
making up the air if we have to, out of hearing.

Poem on the First Day of Spring

A new dead child has come to play
in my backyard with my daughter
summoned from limbo. My wife, gone five years,
hovers above them, while I am called
to set up swings and sandbox I assembled
forty years ago, a season of anticipation.

One step into the yard, it's all here again.
Is death that much at home in me
I go back quickly, hands on the wrench,
the nails and hammer, effortlessly returned to work?

The girls, five maybe, gleeful to be together,
each grab a swing, while my Jacki retrieves
the smile I remember, answering mine,
moments like this we shared our children.
Who is the new dead child? Neither of us cares.

Jacki sits on the sandbox edge
balancing her new, resurrected flesh.
And I step backward, admiring
our magnolia tree I planted forty years ago
to celebrate our nameless daughter's coming.
It should have bloomed the first time that spring
but refused until we accepted the stillbirth.
Today wind takes direction from the blossomings.

And now they're gone. The dead are like this.
A moment here, then, my next breath, no one.
They have no need of me. They come, they go.
Memory, you dull, sequestered thing,
here, there, indecipherable perishings.

An Ordinary Summer in New Orleans

Nothing much here to make into a day—
streaks at the window calling themselves in,

the sky beyond them churning, cloud-on-cloud
dragons, castles, a child's picture book,

the spaces between clouds, before, after
that emptiness where everything begins.

And then the void. When I stare into it—
I may be here seconds, I may be here all day—

the gods begin their music I can't hear.
I know it's there, I'm their accompaniment.

When I am lost in weather I make up—
who knows whether it's snowing in Rangoon—

I tell myself I'm counting flake-on-flake,
and leave by clouds I came to, leaving me,
and return by way of Xanadu, on course.

Faster, Faster

All night the trees have prayed for me
and not because I asked them to.

Now, first light, I am waking to their finishings,
the window shaking with the day's gold winds.

Listen, when I allow my ancient man to run,
to trespass on modernity awhile,

(I'm running as I write this), he gathers leaves,
descents from the magnolia in my yard,

night and day falling, all seasons falling there.
Watch while I press those prayers against my face,

the waxy, sea-deep green an ocean floor
of promises. What will today make of me,

leaves I'm reading here? What portents
of still-to-be fulfilled Old World miracles

churn in the grasses shifting winds beneath my feet?

Poem in the Third Week of Advent

And so it is, by resonance of grace
in my soul's eye, through the vision of darkness,
between moonset and sunrise, they begin
again
their journey from eternity, the three
again,
indivisible in imagination.

The Magi imagine me. And God is being born.

Mornings like these, I stand up to myself.
I ask the day for blessings as they come
again,
once more in these trees' obeisance as I pass
beneath them on my morning walk, bowing.

Maybe just one of them will choose me, scatter
the light they never question through the small fire I carry,
their light that gathers at the tops of trees.
The Three Kings setting out. That eternity.
Again.

Keats and Company

How calm it is here now, before the day.
My winds and I stand, waiting for the dawn.
When the sun comes, first light between the trees,
I'll have to start to give it a new name,
my breath a little song, mending, breaking,
lyrics fitted to the scores of morning birds.

We won't ask how long our medley lasts, will we?
My signature written on this morning's wind
writes and rewrites as if I could carve
my name on the frieze of immortality
besides Keats, his own writ-in-water.

Just a Little Exultation

The difference between prayer and poetry?
That difference between thunderhead and flood.
When the earth lifts, blade-on-blade,
its rampant expectations to the morning.
such inveterate green shimmerings!

I walk out into the waiting.
How impatient the world is
to see what I can carve from it,
just one among the scores of lies
I tell myself to stay alive, exultant.
And look, the shattered blossoms
on the shower-slathered sidewalk
my next-door neighbor's magnolia scattered
rise, I swear, to greet me, unexpectantly.
Yes, the blossoms, on faith, assure me
the sky ruptures
only for my company,
and the clouds, invisible now,
will maintain necessary, expected unfamiliar resurrections—

Fra Angelico, *The Annunciation*, 1432–1434

Light from my chosen star will come to me
in morning prayer, but only if I beg,
desperate like the unfortunate I met
yesterday morning. New Orleans 8 a.m.
corner Claiborne and. Carrollton.
He lifted both palms up, That's how I pray
we're brotherbodies Fate estranged—

I'm sure the stars pray in dazzling choirs
or singly, hands clasped to their chests
like Fra's angel, kneeling, right knee bent,
facing Mary, supernal light gracing the porticos.
This visit that might have changed the world.

If only I could transcribe the painting's beautifuls!
But here I am, exhausted as if I'd spent the night
sleeping in the park the way he has to,
ashamed of the comparison but praying this
on one knee beside my bed, asking myself,
asking the morning star and you and You,
why did I drive by, not giving him a dime?
How dare I try to compare myself, twice,
to the angel, to him, both, I'm twice-ashamed.
And, say it, afraid, twice-afraid to write this.

To Continue

August 29, 2021, Anniversary of Hurricane Katrina, 2005

This is the place where the gods stood today
when they passed by my house to check on me,
to see I was ok after Hurricane Ida.
They left a gold shadow on the morning grass.
I bend to it, picking up the paper,
The Times-Picayune of New Orleans
with a double headline: "Delta Variant-Hurricane."
I don't appreciate the mangled humor.
One of my friends lost his house and grandmother.

I let my right hand pass over the holy burn
and, without asking, the skin assumes some fire
in forefinger and thumb, enough to calm me.

Maybe tomorrow in the other three fingers
I will find the ghost of some new gods,
newer even than the ones I made up
today just to keep getting me through.

Wonder's Other Side

The blue hydrangea
my neighbor's front yard
blooming all seasons
tight blue mysteries
as if the whole sky
came down in one rush
unasked for faces
undecipherable
and multiple gods
answering to this blue
to keep me on edge
stunned in my belief.

Meanwhile my neighbor
comes and goes his car
reflecting the clouds
a green he waxes
Sunday afternoons
crucifix dangling
between his biceps
you can have that thing
he said yesterday
you like it so much
oh I can't but thanks
I said in wonder
I wouldn't know how
to take care of this.

Gracelight

—for David Rowan

My son-in-law, addiction counselor,
tells me to give the unhoused nothing when they ask.

I grace their palms anyway. It gives me hope.
We don't know how many friends may die tonight.

nor which seeds we plant will split a rock.
We never know how many days we have

nor how many stars break up under our feet.
He says they need therapy, but they give me grace.

wandering the highway beside my house,
poor as the poor Christ offered blessings.

Did I just say that? Dare to bring in Christ?
I can't let my son-in-law know what I'm doing,

And I will never show him this poem, ever.

Treatise on the Dark

It's not as if the Dark can't learn our names.
It can. In milliseconds. Dark loves to bide Dark's time,
peepholing while we stroll the hardware store
for that new screw to tighten the door handle.
Dark loves door handles, it grips each in its fist.
Dark loves screw heads, churning the vortex deeper.
Dark loves doors most, exploding right through them.

But equally the Dark loves noon—for argument—
the innocency of that hour which is all light
some will call gods or Christ or whatever,
Dark says. Look, one of us was here first, Light,
since even while you shine and blind and symbolize
Dark says, you, Light, are perishing.

Dark watched us this morning at the mirror
while we knotted our tie, fastened our earrings.
It stood behind the mirror, thirsty, hungry.
Not this week, Dark said, and slipped away awhile,
a little while, to postpone, a little while longer—

Ontological

I am the first of the sky's monotonies,
the star you cannot pick up from the grass

after I've fallen, eons of fallings are there.
I move too fast toward taking shape

in figurations of the morning clouds
dispersing when you try to give us names.

I am the name behind the names, remembering
my origins at the formation of the world.

Christians would call me Christ, I'll take that name
an instant or two, beside Big Bang or Chaos.

But I have others with more jagged edges,
more spiders moiling in the fucking box,

more chance transcendence in a saint's appearance,
more worms ensouled in a crow's shot guts.

Try me: I am the sea's greatest monotonies,
the sea behind me, the sea above, around,

the sea, which is entirely me and not,
the gift of giving given by the gods,

the gift of breath I give you to take back,
the sea, which is a wave of me, breaking,

the sea, which is a metaphor, but I am not.

Midas and Midas

What did I find in love's high offices,
the lives of saints, the words priests drilled in me?

I've found more love in parlance of the stones
as they ring one another's melodies
mornings I'm jogging them, the river road.

Antiphonal, that's what I'd call this luck
I've drawn out of the music of least things,

the lesser burden, the least kind of weight:
first I found a rat skin in the sewer grate,
then droppings of the sparrows shone, turned gold.

What do you think of my perplexities,
Constant Reader, you whom I call up

out of the stones, you who have walked with me
down streets we haven't even found names for yet
and never will, maybe—and will we care?

You're at the window as I tell you this,
you're watching rain, you are rain itself.

New Orleans rain, sun-shot, rain Midas gold.

Landscape with the Ascent of Icarus

But once he fell, those stones he found along the floor
the ocean swept clean for his entrance
swam up, attached to his shoulders, new appendages.
Somehow when he ascended, they were little hidden wings.
He rubs them—oh, you know he's me—
they prick and itch, and greedy to poke, sprout,
wilder, wilder, need to be trimmed back, right this minute
to nub-yokes fitted to my shoulder blades.
When I get on my knees the trimming works.
Yes, praying on the cold floor is taking care of it.

Song That Can Only Be for You

When I begin again the stars align,
the ones I find buried in my steps' macadam,

and the shrubs stand taller to address the sycamore,
where it is said the souls of the dead keep

their being in such eternity as the trees know.
And all of this in my backyard. Which shrub

will I be given, that dwarf pine by the fence,
blown there to teach me my place among giants?

Or something smaller when I begin again?

When I begin again the light at midnight,
if I ask, can shine like noon across the grass.

I bend and stoop to carry so much radiance
I pick up as I go and then release.

It's always in releasing that the possible can grow
to stand behind me, before, at either side.

Which light belongs to stars they've gifted me
to give back, which ones are my birthright?

Why ask, when I begin again again?

Obit

for Billy Sothern

It really doesn't matter to the wind,
the sun, dancing together my front yard,
dancing a kind of joyous coupling,
a silent music, adagio of gold
playing the trees, sprung to new life,
crepe myrtle, oak, willow, trinity
I have to bow to, however badly here . . .

It doesn't matter that my friend
hung himself yesterday, that I found out
checking my phone for messages from friends
after drowning a half hour in Facebook.
It doesn't matter, it really doesn't matter—

Today I will go out, buy some chrysanthemums,
flowers of a corresponding gold
to the New Orleans sun, that radiance.
I'm trying to bring down the sky again,
hours flecked with the gold of passing,
already as I speak their triumph
occluded by cloud cover at ten o'clock.
I'm going to station that gold
on my front steps, all three,
let the sky walk up and down
in potted plants' circumferences
as if grief could be encircled,
as if I could bring him back a moment—
here, there, in the days to come,
wondering that gold's continuance.

Wonderments

—our longest sun sets at right descensions and makes but winter
arches, and therefore it cannot be long before we lie down in
darkness, and have our light in ashes; since the brother of death daily
haunts us with dying mementos, and time, that grows old in itself,
bids us no long duration

—Sir Thomas Browne, *Hydriotaphia, Urn Burial*

A day of quiet wonder in my hands
holding nothing but bewilderment
at the green world knocking on my window—
I am alive! fresh from harrowing
my address book, a kind of columbarium
page after page, the too-soon,
too-many dead. Bob, heart attack,
at fifty-five, Nancy, throat cancer, sixty,
Carolyn, double-vaccinated, Covid, seventy,
all of them here, then a moment, suddenly—

suddenly, even the long death of my mother
I watched, while I sat beside her
weeks, with the hospice nurse, dazed,
then suddenly, I saw her eyes glazed over,
a yellow glare of translucent cellophane
all her gaze, transfixed on mine
as if she'd seen enough of me for a while.—

In a minute now I will go out
into the terrible gift of the sun
just one of my unaccountable, unasked fors—

If I disbelieved in coincidence,
which I do not, I might think it coincidental,

not heaven-sent, that this the first
day of spring and this afternoon
I will need to buy a new, gold-embossed
leather-bound address book,
if they still sell such antiquities,
one which will outlast my being here.

In the life to come, I believe
I will look back on this, look down on this,
wondering while I was here
how long I thought I might need
that address book, its inchoate,
unfingered, immaculate, sheer white pages—